The Witches
by Roald Dahl

Adapted for the stage
by

David Wood

Samuel French — London
New York - Toronto - Hollywood

The Witches

Grandmother (JANET WHITESIDE) tells Boy (KAREN BRIFFETT) all about Witches

THE WITCHES

The Boy-Mouse (KAREN BRIFFETT) convinces Bruno (ADAM STAF-FORD) that he, too, has turned into a mouse

THE WITCHES

The Witches was first performed at the Lyceum Theatre, Sheffield on 8th October 1992 and on tour, including a West End season for Christmas at the Duke of York's Theatre. The play was presented by James Woods and Justin Savage for Clarion Productions, with the following cast:

Boy	**Karen Briffett**
Grandmother	**Janet Whiteside**
Display Witch/Witch One/Voice of Maid	**Caroline High**
Lawyer/Hotel Doorman/Head Waiter	**Terence Frisch**
Sailor/Doctor/Mr Jenkins/Head Chef	**Eric Potts**
Nurse/Waitress	**Emma Jay**
Tree-House Witch/Mrs Jenkins/Witch Two	**Susannah Bray**
Bruno Jenkins/Frog/Second Chef	**Adam Stafford**
Grand High Witch	**Dorothy Ann Gould**
Waiter	**Kenneth Collard**

The Witches at the Annual General Meeting were recruited locally at each theatre

Director	**David Wood**
Designer	**Susie Caulcutt**
Illusions	**Paul Kieve**
Lighting Designer	**Simon Courtenay-Taylor**
Movement	**Sheila Falconer**
Music Composer and Supervisor	**Peter Pontzen**
Musical Director	**Cliff Atkinson**
Puppets	**John Thirtle**
Sound Designer	**Mike Furness**

COPYRIGHT INFORMATION

(See also page iv)

Cast of Characters with Suggested Doubling

Companies with more actors available need not use these doubling suggestions. It would, however, be difficult to perform the play with less than ten principal actors.

Actor 1	Boy
Actor 2	Grandmother
Actor 3	Display Witch/Witch One/Voice of Maid
Actor 4	Lawyer/Hotel Doorman/Head Waiter
Actor 5	Sailor/Doctor/Mr Jenkins/Head Chef
Actor 6	Tree-House Witch/ Mrs Jenkins/Witch Two
Actor 7	Bruno Jenkins/Frog/Second Chef
Actor 8	Grand High Witch
Actor 9	Nurse/Waitress
Actor 10	Waiter/Puppeteer

Fifteen or so Witches (no individual lines)
Three or Four Diners in the Restaurant (can be doubled by Witches)
A Musician

ACKNOWLEDGEMENTS

Photographs
The photographs in this Acting Edition are from the original production and are reproduced by permission of the photographer, Dee Conway.

Music
Optional incidental music, composed by Peter Pontzen for the original production, is available from Samuel French Ltd.

Cover Illustration
The cover illustration for this play is reproduced by kind permission of the artist, Quentin Blake, whose copyright it remains. Enquiries regarding its use, for whatever purpose, must be addressed to the artist c/o A.P Watt, 20 John Street, WC1N 2DR

INTRODUCTION

Adapting *The Witches* for the stage was quite a challenge! Although the story is a marvellously theatrical one, the effects required to make its magical content convincing were somewhat daunting.

For the original production we employed the skills of an illusionist and a puppeteer, and companies contemplating their own productions are advised to do the same.

Unfortunately the rules of the Magic Circle make it impossible to disclose the secrets we employed, but I hope this will not prevent companies finding their own solutions.

What I can say is that it was necessary for our designer to work closely with the illusionist and puppeteer to create a set which, while looking innocent, incorporated the furniture and props necessary to achieve the illusions. This prevented the production looking like a magic show!

I can assure prospective producers that the effort required to stage this play will be worthwhile. The effect of this dramatic tale on audiences of all ages was truly memorable.

David Wood

The Hotel Restaurant

SYNOPSIS OF SCENES

ACT I

    Grandmother's Parlour (Norway)
    A Ship's Rail
    The Tree-House
    The Exterior of the Entrance to the Hotel Magnificent
    The Hotel Ballroom

ACT II

    Corner of Ballroom (Giant-Scale)
    Two Giant Steps
    Grandmother's Hotel Bedroom
    Under the Grand High Witch's Bed (Giant-Scale)
    The Hotel Restaurant
    The Hotel Kitchen
    The Hotel Restaurant
    Grandmother's Parlour (Norway)

The action of the play takes place in Norway, at sea and in England, in particular at the Hotel Magnificent, Bournemouth

For Pookie, who is
anything but a witch
and everything to me

ACT I

As the House Lights go down, the gentle purr of a car engine is heard. The volume increases to an engine roar as the CURTAIN *rises on a darkened stage*

A sudden screech of brakes. A crash

A single Light picks out Boy, downstage

Boy Christmas holidays. Winter sunshine. Happy. North of Oslo. Papa driving. Mama beside him. Me in the back. Icy road. Skidding, sliding, out of control. Off the road. Tumbling. Into a rocky ravine. (*He calls*) Mama! Papa! No!

He turns and runs to Grandmother's parlour

There is an easy chair, a small table with a lamp. This all creates a cosy atmosphere. Grandmother is waiting. She enfolds Boy in her arms. She comforts him as he sobs

Grandmother Sob your heart out, darling Boy. Grandmamma's here.
Boy What are we going to do now?
Grandmother You will stay here with me. And I will look after you.
Boy Aren't I going back to England?
Grandmother No. I could never do that. Heaven shall take my soul, but Norway shall keep my bones.

They continue hugging. Grandmother turns to the audience

As the days passed, time began to heal the hurt.

She leads Boy to her chair. She sits. He kneels at her feet. A clock ticks

Each evening I told him stories of summer holidays when I was young. (*To Boy*) We used to row out in a boat and wave to the shrimpboats on their way home. They would stop and give us a handful of shrimps each, still warm from having just been cooked. We peeled them and gobbled them up. The head was the best part.

Boy looks interested

Boy The head?
Grandmother You squeeze it between your teeth and suck out the inside. (*She demonstrates with relish*) It's marvellous.
Boy Uggggh! It's horrible!

He is enjoying the horror

Grandmother (*lighting a thin black cigar*) Horrible things can be exciting, Boy. Take ... witches.
Boy Witches? With silly black hats and black cloaks riding on broom-sticks.
Grandmother No. They're for fairy-tales. Very tame. I'm talking of *real* witches.
Boy *Real* witches?
Grandmother Real witches dress in ordinary clothes and look very much like ordinary women. That's why they're so hard to catch.
Boy But why should we want to catch them?
Grandmother Because, my darling Boy, they are evil. They hate children. They get the same pleasure from squelching a child as you get from eating a plateful of strawberries and thick cream.
Boy Squelching?
Grandmother She chooses a victim, softly stalks it. Closer and closer, then... phwisst! ... she swoops. Sparks fly. Flames leap. Oil boils. Rats howl. Skin shrivels and the child disappears. Squelched.
Boy Disappears?

Grandmother Not always. Sometimes the child is transformed into something else. Like little Birgit Svenson who lived across the road from us. One day she started growing feathers all over her body. Within a month she had turned intò a large white chicken. Her parents kept her for years in a pen in the garden. She even laid eggs.

Boy What colour eggs?

Grandmother Brown ones. Biggest eggs I've ever seen. Her mother made omelettes out of them. Delicious they were.

Boy Are you being truthful, Grandmamma? Really and truly truthful? Not pulling my leg.

Grandmother My darling Boy, you won't last long in this world if you don't know how to spot a witch when you see one.

Boy Then tell me. Please!

Grandmother takes a large tome from the table and opens it to show Boy a picture

Music. As Grandmother finds the page, the Display Witch is seen. She is isolated in a pool of light and looks like an ordinary woman

(*Looking at the book*) She doesn't look like a witch.

Grandmother Of course not. If witches looked like witches we could round them all up and put them in the meat-grinder. But look, there's a clue. She's wearing gloves.

Boy Mama used to wear gloves.

Grandmother Not in the summer, when it's hot. Not in the house. A witch does.

Boy Why?

Grandmother Because she doesn't have fingernails.

The Display Witch, almost in choreographed slow motion, removes a glove

She has thin, curvy claws, like a cat.

The Display Witch gestures threateningly with her claws

Boy Uggggh!

Grandmother Second clue. She wears a wig. A real witch is always bald.

The Display Witch removes her wig revealing a bald head

> Not a single hair grows on her head

Boy Horrid.

Grandmother Disgusting.

The Display Witch begins to scratch her bald head

> And the wig gives her nasty sores on the head. Wig-rash, it's called. And it doesn't half itch.

Boy What else, Grandmamma?

Grandmother Big nose-holes.

The Display Witch raises her head and flares her nostrils

Boy What for?

Grandmother To sniff out the stink-waves of children.

Boy I don't give out stink-waves, do I?

Grandmother Not to me, you don't. To me you smell like raspberries and cream. But to a witch you smell — all children smell — like fresh dogs' droppings.

Boy Dogs' droppings? I don't believe it.

Grandmother So, if you see a woman holding her nose as she passes you in the street, that woman could easily be a witch. Now, look at her feet.

Boy Nothing special about them.

Grandmother Wrong. She has no toes.

The Display Witch takes off a shoe revealing a stockinged stub

Boy Uggggh!

Grandmother And last but not least, a witch has blue spit.

The Display Witch smiles for the first time, revealing a haze of blue teeth. She cackles menacingly and disappears as the Lights fade on the Display Witch

Grandmother closes the book

So, my darling Boy, now you know.

Boy leaves Grandmother and comes downstage

Boy Next day talk of witches was forgotten. A man came.

The Lawyer enters, with a briefcase, and holding a document

Something to do with my parents' will.

Lawyer (*to Grandmother*) They insist the boy continues his education in England. After all, he was born there.

Grandmother Very well.

Boy enters the scene

Boy Grandmamma, you can't send me away!

Grandmother Of course not. I'll come to England too.

Boy But you don't want to go. You said so.

Grandmother It is important to respect the wishes of the parents. (*To the Lawyer*) Is it not?

Lawyer I'm sorry, madam.

Grandmother Term begins soon. No time to waste.

The Lights fade as the scene clears. A ship's hooter fills the air, followed by seagulls' cries and the sound of the sea

The Lights come up on a ship's rail. Boy and Grandmother, wearing topcoats, lean on the rail

Boy Is that England, Grandmamma?

Grandmother The docks of Newcastle, yes. Not the most romantic of landing places.

A Sailor enters and passes through the scene

Boy Grandmamma...

Grandmother Yes?

Boy Are there any witches in England?

Grandmother Of course. Every country has its own Secret Society of Witches.

Boy I'm sure I won't meet one.

Grandmother I sincerely hope you won't. English witches are probably the most vicious in the whole world.

Boy What do they do?

Grandmother Their favourite ruse is to mix up a powder that turns a child into a creature all the grown-ups hate.

Boy Such as?

Grandmother A slug. Then the grown-ups step on the slug and squish it without knowing it's a child, *their* child maybe.

Boy That's awful.

Grandmother That's English witches for you.

Boy These ... Societies of Witches. Do they have meetings? Like our Chess Society at school?

Grandmother They have an annual meeting, attended by the Grand High Witch of all the World.

Boy Grand High Witch? Who's she?

The Sailor passes through again

Sailor (*shouting*) Prepare for disembarcation if you please.

Grandmother ushers Boy away

Grandmother Come on!

Boy But, Grandmamma...

Grandmother exits

As the scene clears, Boy steps forward

Soon life was back to sort of normal. We lived in our old house and I went back to school. One Saturday afternoon, when my friend Timmy was in bed with 'flu, I decided to do some work on the tree-house we were building at the bottom of the garden ...

The Lights come up on the tree-house. Birdsong. Boy climbs up and starts nailing a plank

Sinister music as the Tree-House Witch enters. She sniffs, her nostrils flared. She traces the scent, looking up to Boy, who works on, unaware. The birdsong stops

Tension mounts as the Witch slowly starts to climb the steps to the tree-house

Boy is still hammering the nail. Just as it seems the Tree-House Witch might reach him, he accidentally drops the hammer with a clatter. The Tree-House Witch retreats a little

Boy descends to fetch his hammer. He picks it up, turns, and suddenly sees the Witch. He stops

Witch (*waving a gloved hand*) Hallo, boy.

She smiles a blue smile

Don't be shy. I have a present for you.

Boy, nervous, starts to climb the steps

Come down out of that tree, boy, and I shall give you the most exciting present you've ever had.

Still looking up at Boy, she produces, perhaps from her handbag, a thin green snake. It coils itself round her forearm

If you come down here, I shall give him to you.

Boy, almost mesmerised by the snake, descends and approaches

It's tame. Come stroke him.

Boy goes to stroke the snake. Suddenly the Tree-House Witch grabs Boy by the arm. A struggle ensues. Then Boy stamps on the Tree-House Witch's foot. She screams with frustration as Boy climbs back up to the tree-house to hide

The Tree-House Witch calms herself, then leaves, cackling horribly

The Lights fade. Time-passing music. An owl hoots

Grandmother (*off*) Boy!

Grandmother enters with a torch

Boy!
Boy (*from the tree-house*) Grandmamma. Up here.
Grandmother Come down at once. It's past your suppertime.
Boy Has that woman gone?
Grandmother What woman?
Boy The woman in the black gloves.

Grandmother is stunned

Grandmother Gloves?
Boy Has she gone?
Grandmother Yes, she's gone. I'm here, my darling.

Boy descends gingerly. Then, trembling, he falls into Grandmother's arms

There, there. I'll look after you.
Boy (*with an effort*) I've seen a witch.

A cackle echoes through the night as the Lights fade

The Lights come up in a small area downstage. Boy steps into the light

Just before the end of the summer term, when Grandmamma and I were looking forward to going back to Norway for the holidays, she fell ill. Very ill.

The Lights come up on another downstage area. A doctor attends Grandmother, slumped in an armchair

Pneumonia. It was touch and go. But Grandmamma was strong. After ten long days she pulled through.

The Doctor leaves Grandmother and a Nurse takes his place

Doctor But she's still weak. Too weak to make the crossing to Norway.
Boy But our holiday ...
Doctor Do you want your Grandmother to die?
Boy Never.
Doctor Then no Norway. But I'll tell you what you can do. Take her to a nice hotel on the south coast of England instead. The sea air would do her good. And stop her smoking those vile black cigars!

He goes

Boy And that's how we came to stay in Bournemouth. At the Hotel Magnificent.

Music plays as Boy exits

The scene changes to the imposing front door of the hotel. Steps rise graciously to the entrance. Traffic noises

As the Lights come up slowly, the hotel Doorman is discovered on duty

Bruno Jenkins enters and stands near the Doorman cheekily imitating his stance and making rude faces

He laughs at the Doorman who is trying not to react to the rudeness. Bruno then sits on the steps and provocatively starts eating a cream bun

A Lady (Witch) enters and tries to climb the steps

Bruno is in her way. She tries to get round him, but he slides himself along the step to block her path

Lady Excuse me.
Bruno (*rudely*) Why? What've you done?
Lady Pardon me?

Bruno Granted.

He laughs

Lady Move, please.
Bruno Shan't. So there.

The Doorman appoaches

Doorman Shift yourself, sunshine.

He pushes Bruno, whose face hits the cream bun

Bruno (*spluttering*) Here!
Doorman Good-day, madam.
Lady Thank you.

   The door is held open by the Doorman. The Lady enters the hotel

Bruno (*to the Doorman*) I'll set my Dad on you.
Doorman (*impassively*) I can't wait.

   Another Lady (Witch) arrives

Good- day, madam. Straight through for the meeting.

   He opens the door. Before the Lady can enter, Mr Jenkins squashes
rudely through

Mr Jenkins (*loudly*) Bruno.
Bruno Yes, Dad.

   The Lady manages to go in

Doorman (*long suffering*) Can I help you, Mr Jenkins?
Mr Jenkins No, you can't. You lot only help if there's a tip at the end of
it. Beat it, Buttons.
Bruno Yes, beat it, Buttons! (*He laughs*)
Doorman As you please, sir.

He goes inside

Mr Jenkins Shut your face, Bruno. Where's your Ma?
Bruno Gone to buy me a doughnut.
Mr Jenkins You'll turn into a doughnut, you fat slob.
Bruno So?
Mr Jenkins Tell your Ma I'm in the bar.

He turns to go

Bruno Getting drunk time, is it, Pa?
Mr Jenkins (*stopping by the door*) What?
Bruno I said "Nearly lunchtime, is it, Pa?"
Mr Jenkins Watch it.

Another Lady (Witch) approaches. The Doorman opens the door from the inside, knocking it into Mr Jenkins

(*To the Doorman*) Watch it.
Doorman (*sweetly*) So sorry, Mr Jenkins.

Mr Jenkins rudely goes inside ahead of the Lady

Mr Jenkins (*to the Lady*) Watch it.
Doorman Good-day, madam. Straight through.

Bruno takes out a magnifying glass and focuses it on a step

Boy enters carrying a box

Boy Hallo, Bruno.
Bruno What you got in there? Something to eat? Give us some.
Boy I've been to the pet shop. Grandmamma gave me some money.
Bruno What've you got?
Boy White mice. I'm going to call them William and Mary.
Bruno Boring. Guess what pets I got.
Boy What?
Bruno Chinchillas and mink.

Boy Oh?
Bruno Gonna make me Ma a fur coat, see.
Boy Oh.

Another Lady (Witch) arrives, steps over Bruno and enters the hotel

Bruno (*concentrating on his magnifying glass now*) Bet my Dad earns
more than yours.
Boy Probably.
Bruno How many cars has he got, your dad?
Boy None.
Bruno Mine's got three.
Boy What are you doing with that magnifying glass?
Bruno Roasting ants.
Boy That's horrible. Stop it.

He tries to grab the magnifying glass

Bruno Here. Get away. Shove off.

A scuffle breaks out

Mrs Jenkins enters carrying a paper bag

Mrs Jenkins Bruno!

She tries to pull the boys apart

(*To Boy*) You great bully. (*She slaps hard an arm which she thinks
belongs to Boy, but which in fact belongs to Bruno*) Lay off my little
Bruno, do you hear?
Bruno (*wailing*) Ow! Mum...
Mrs Jenkins (*going to Bruno and brushing him down*) Look at you, your
shorts are all grubby.
Bruno He tried to nick my magnifying glass.
Mrs Jenkins (*to Boy*) You keep away from my little Bruno, d'you hear?
(*To Bruno*) There's your doughnut, treasure.
Bruno (*taking it greedily*) Ask him what's in that box, Ma.
Mrs Jenkins Why? (*To Boy*) Have you nicked that 'n' all?

Boy No. It's William and Mary.
Mrs Jenkins What d'you mean, William and Mary? Give us a look.

She lifts the lid. A mouse's head pops up

Ahhhhhhh! Mice! Aaaaaaaaaaaaah!

She runs up the steps and into the hotel screaming

Bruno (*roaring with laughter, calling after her*) Pa's in the bar, Ma. (*But she has gone*) Silly old witch.
Boy (*alert*) What did you say?
Bruno Nothing.
Boy I'd better go and see Grandmamma.

The Doorman opens the door for him. He enters the hotel

Another Lady enters (Witch). She is welcomed by the Doorman and enters the hotel

Bruno sits on the steps and starts eating the doughnut and scooping out jam on his finger

The Doorman descends the steps, pretending not to notice Bruno. He takes a deep breath or two of fresh air

Sinister music as another Lady (The Grand High Witch) enters

The Doorman turns and sees her

Doorman Good-day, madam.
Grand High Witch (*charming*) Good-day. Is this the correct hotel for the Annual General Meeting of the Royal Society for the Prevention of Cruelty to Children?
Doorman It is indeed, madam. Welcome.

He ascends the steps and holds the door open

The Grand High Witch starts to ascend the steps, but suddenly stops. She starts sniffing, as genteely as possible, and turns to see the source of the stink-waves, which is Bruno. She approaches him

Grand High Witch Vell, hallo, little man.
Bruno Eh?
Grand High Witch You are liking your doughnut, yes?

Bruno nods

But vot happens ven it is finished? Vould you like some chocolate?

She hands him a bar of chocolate

Bruno (*enthusiastically*) Yeah.

He breaks off a piece and eats it

Grand High Witch Good?
Bruno Great.
Grand High Witch Vould you like some more?
Bruno Yeah.
Grand High Witch I vill give you six more chocolate bars like that if you vill meet me in the ballroom of this hotel at tventy-five-past three.
Bruno Six bars! I'll be there.

The Grand High Witch ascends the steps and enters the hotel, the door held open by the Doorman

You bet I'll be there!

The Lights fade on Bruno, stuffing his face. Music as the scene changes to the ballroom where there are mirrors and a chandelier, a raised platform, a door and some chairs. There is a folding screen downstage to one side

(N.B In the original production, the scene change, in "blue wash" light, was orchestrated by the Doorman, assisted by a Waiter and Waitress, who exited, not through the ballroom door, but offstage as though to a staff area)

As the Lights come up, Boy, carrying his box containing William and Mary, enters through the door, impressed by the grand room

Boy After lunch, Grandmamma had her rest, while I found a secret spot in a colossal empty room called the Ballroom. The perfect place for some mouse circus training.

(N.B As this point, in the original production, the Doorman, Waiter and Waitress re-entered and set up chairs for the forthcoming meeting. Music accompanied this. Boy hid behind the screen as they entered, then re-emerged once the chairs were set and the Doorman, Waiter and Waitress had exited)

(To the tune of "Entry of the Gladiators") Da da dadelade da da da da, da da dadelade da da da da ... Ladies and gentlemen, the world famous White Mouse Circus proudly presents William, the wizard of the tightrope! Da da! *(He shows William on a tight rope. He holds a piece of cake in one hand)* Now then, William, here's a tasty piece of fruitcake, come and get it! Come on, come on, good mouse, good mouse! ... Yes! *(He gives William a nibble of cake)* Now back to the centre ... now Ladies and Gentlemen, William will somersault on the high trapeze! One, two, three, hup! One, two, three, hup! Bravo!!

Suddenly the Ballroom is flooded with light from the chandelier. Boy hides downstage of the screen. He reacts with mounting curiosity, watching through a gap in the screen

To music, the Doorman enters and ushers in a troupe of ladies (Witches) who noisily babble and ad-lib the following to each other

Witches *(variously)* Oh hallo, Beatrice. What an adorable dress! ...Agatha, how lovely to see you....Have you had a good journey?...Come and sit next to me, Millie dear....I haven't seen you since the last meeting. *Etc.*

They arrange themselves, seated facing the platform. As they talk, some scratch their necks with gloved hands

Eventually the Doorman calls for attention

Doorman Ladies of the Royal Society for the Prevention of Cruelty to
Children, pray welcome your President.

*Enthusiastic applause. The Grand High Witch enters in style to a
fanfare. She mounts the platform. The Doorman exits*

A Witch locks the door

*(N.B In the original production Witch One was presented as an acolyte
of the Grand High Witch, locking the door, helping the Grand High Witch
by receiving her wig and mask on a cushion, holding up the recipe on a
scroll etc. This is not essential but helped the Grand High Witch achieve
a regal manner)*

*Slowly the Grand High Witch removes her wig and then mask, revealing
a wizened, horrible, rotting face. The other Witches watch in awe*

Grand High Witch You may rrree-moof your vigs, and get some fresh
air into your spotty scalps.

With sighs of relief, the Witches reveal their bald heads

Vitches of Inkland. Miserrrable vitches. Useless lazy vitches. You are
a heap of idle good-for-nothing vurms!

A murmur of concern amongst the Witches

As I am eating my lunch, I am looking out of the vindow at the beach.
And vot am I seeing? I am seeing a rrreevolting sight, which is putting
me off my food. Hundreds of rrrotten rrrepulsive children. Playing on
the sand. Vye have you not got rrrid of them? Vye?

No response

You vill do better.
Witches We will, your Grandness. We will do better.
Grand High Witch My orders are that every single child in Inkland shall
be rrrubbed out, sqvashed, sqvirted, sqvittered and frittered before I

come here again in vun year's time.

A gasp through the audience

Witch Two *All* of them? We can't possibly wipe out *all* of them.
Grand High Witch Who said that? Who dares to argue vith me? (*She points dramatically at Witch Two*) It vos you, vos it not?

Witch Two stands, gasping in fright

Witch Two I didn't mean it, your Grandness.
Grand High Witch Come here.

She beckons. Witch Two, mesmerised, ascends the platform

Witch Two I didn't mean to argue, your Grandness. I was just talking to myself. I swear it.
Grand High Witch   A vitch who dares to say I'm wrrrrong
                         Vill not be vith us very long!
Witch Two Forgive me, your Grandness.
Grand High Witch   A stupid vitch who answers back
                         Must burn until her bones are black!
Witch Two No! No! Spare me!

Staring at Witch Two, the Grand High Witch gestures. Sparks fly. Smoke rises

Aaaaaaaaaaah!

Witch Two disappears

A great sigh through the audience. Boy reacts too

Grand High Witch I hope nobody else is going to make me cross today.

Witch One finds the smouldering remnants of Witch Two's clothes and holds them up

Frrrizzled like a frrritter. Cooked like a carrot. You vill never see her again. Now vee can get down to business.

A rhythmic pulse conveys an ominous mood. The following sequence grows in intensity

Grand High Witch	Down vith children! Do them in!
Witches	Boil their bones and fry their skin!
Grand High Witch	Bish them, sqvish them, bash them, mash them!
Witches	Break them, shake them, slash them, smash them!

Grand High Witch I am having a plan. A giganticus plan!

Witches She is having a plan. A giganticus plan!

Grand High Witch You vill buy sveetshops.

Witches We will buy sweetshops.

Grand High Witch You vill fill them high vith luscious sveets and tasty chocs!

Witches Luscious sweets and tasty chocs!

Grand High Witch You vill have a Great Gala Opening vith free sveets and chocs for every child!

Witches Free sweets and chocs for every child!

Witch One is carried away with enthusiasm

Witch One I will *poison* the sweets and *poison* the chocs and wipe out the children like weasels.

Silence. The rhythmic pulse stops

Grand High Witch You vill do no such thing. You brainless bogvumper! Poison them and you vill be caught in five minutes flat. No. Vee vitches are vurrrking only vith magic!

Witches (*building*) Magic! Magic! Magic!

Grand High Witch You vill be filling every choc and every sveet vith my latest and grrreatest magic formula.

A sigh of admiration as she produces a potion bottle

Formula Eighty-Six Delayed Action Mouse-Maker!

Applause. The Grand High Witch reveals a board or scroll with "Formula Eighty-Six Delayed-Action Mouse-Maker" written on it, followed by the recipe

Take down the recipe.

The Witches take out pads and pencils

You vill notice some unusual ingredients: a grrruntle's egg; the claw of a crrrab-crrruncher; the beak of a blabbersnitch; the snout of a grrrobblesqvirt and the tongue of a catsprrringer. Mix them vith forty-five mouse's tails fried in hair-oil till they are crrrisp.

Witch One What do we do with the mice who have had their tails chopped off, your Grandness?

Grand High Witch You simmer them in frog-juice for vun hour. Then you add two secret ingredients. The wrrrong end of a telescope boiled soft ...

Witch One What's that for, O Brainy One?

Grand High Witch To make a child very small you look at him through the wrrrong end of a telescope, do you not?

Witch One (*to the others*) She's a wonder. Who else would have thought of that.

Grand High Witch And finally, to cause the delayed action, rrroast in the oven vun alarm-clock set to go off at nine o'clock in the morning.

Witch One A stroke of genius!

Grand High Witch Inject vun droplet of the formula in each sveet or choc, open your shop, and as the children pour in on their vay home from school...

She chants the following rhyme

> Crrram them full of sticky eats,
> Send them home still guzzling sveets,
> And in the morning little fools
> Go marching off to separate schools.

A Witch bangs a gong or a bell rings nine times

> A girl feels sick and goes all pale.

She yells, "Hey, look! I've grrrown a tail!
A boy who's standing next to her
Screams, "Help! I think I'm grrrowing fur!"
Another shouts, "Vee look like frrreaks!
There's viskers growing on our cheeks!"
A boy who vos extremely tall
Cries out,"Vot's wrong? I'm grrrowing small!"
Four tiny legs begin to sprrrout
From everybody rrround about.
And all at vunce, all in a trrrice,
There are no children! Only mice!
The teachers cry, "Vot's going on?
Oh, vhere have all the children gone?"
Then suddenly the mice they spot,
Fetch mousetrrraps strrrong and kill the lot!
They sveep the dead mice all away
And all us vitches shout

All   Hooray!

They rise to a big finish

Down vith children! Do them in!
Boil their bones and fry their skin!
Bish them, sqvish them, bash them, mash them!
Brrreak them, shake them, slash them, smash
                them!

The Witches, jumping up, cheer wildly. They sit again. The Grand High Witch acknowledges their appreciation

Suddenly Witch One leaps up and points to the back of the platform

Witch One Look! Look! Mice!

Two white mice are progressing from one side to the other. They stop nervously, looking about

Boy (*seeing them through the gap in the screen*) Oh no! William and Mary!

Witch One Our leader has done it to show us! The Brainy One has turned two children to mice!

The Grand High Witch has seen the mice. The other Witches start to applaud

Grand High Witch Qviet!

She approaches the mice, who stop moving. Music for tension

These mice are nothing to do with me. These mice are *pet* mice, qvite obviously belonging to some repellent little child in this hotel.

She chases the mice, stamping her feet

The mice scurry away and disappear

Witch One (*menacingly*) A child! A filthy child. We'll sniff him out.

The Witches start sniffing and some move ominously towards the screen. Boy stiffens

The music builds. Then, in the nick of time, there is a knock on the door. The Witches react

Bruno (*outside the door*) Hey! Let me in!

More knocks

Grand High Witch Qvick, vitches. Vigs on!

The Witches hurry to make themselves respectable

Bruno (*outside the door*) Hurry up! Twenty-five past three you said.
Grand High Witch Vitches. Vatch this demonstrrration. Earlier today I am giving a chocolate bar vith formula added to a smelly boy.
Bruno (*outside the door*) Where's them chocolate bars you promised? I'm here to collect! Dish 'em out!
Grand High Witch Not only smelly but grrreedy. The formula is timed

for half past three.

She puts on her wig, but not her face mask

Let him in.

Witch One unlocks the door

Bruno enters and approaches

The Grand High Witch keeps her back towards him

(*Soft and gentle*) Darling little man. I have your chocolate all rrready for you. Do come and say hallo to all these lovely ladies.

Bruno ascends the platform. The Witch re-locks the door

Bruno OK, where's my chocolate? Six bars you said.
Grand High Witch (*checking her watch*) Thirty seconds to go.
Bruno What?

He receives no reply

What the heck's going on?
Grand High Witch Twenty seconds!
Bruno (*getting suspicious*) Gimme the chocolate and let me out of here.
Grand High Witch Fifteen seconds!
Bruno (*looking at the Witches*) Will one of you crazy punks kindly tell me what all this is about?
Grand High Witch Ten seconds!

She turns her face to Bruno, who reacts with a terrified scream

Witches Nine ... eight ... seven ... six ... five ... four ... three ... two ... one ... zero!
Grand High Witch Vee have ignition.

An alarm rings. Strange lighting effects as Bruno jumps and yells. He jumps onto a small table, then hops about waving his arms. Then he falls silent and stiffens

Tension music

> This smelly brrrat, this fithy scum
> This horrid little louse
> Vill very soon become
> A lovely little MOUSE!

A flash. Smoke. Music. Bruno appears to shrink; his head darts about like a mouse; his hands, like paws, brush imaginary whiskers

He disappears

In his place on the table-top, a mouse scampers to and fro

Witches (*applauding*) Bravo! She's done it! It works! It's fantastic! *Etc., etc.*

The Grand High Witch shoos the mouse, which appears to make a hurried exit through the Witches, who react

Grand High Witch Vitches, I vill meet you all for dinner at eight. Before dinner, any ancient vuns who can no longer climb high trrrees in search of grrruntles' eggs for the formula may come to my rrroom. I have prrrepared for you (*she shows a tiny bottle*) a bottle each, containing a limited qvantity. Five hundred doses.

Witches (*led by Witch One*) Thank you, thank you, your Grandness. How thoughtful.

Grand High Witch Room Four-Five-Four. Any qvestions?

Witch One One, O Brainy One. What happens if one of the chocolates we are giving away in our shop gets eaten by a grown-up?

Grand High Witch That's just too bad for the grown-up. This meeting is over.

The Witches start to go

Behind the screen Boy relaxes, relieved. He stands up and stretches. He rubs his aching knees

Suddenly ...

Witch One (*shouting*) Wait! Hold everything.

She flares her nostrils, sniffing eagerly. Her face turns towards the screen. Tension music. The Witches freeze and listen

Witch One (*following the scent*) Dog's droppings. I've got a whiff of fresh dogs' droppings.
Grand High Witch Vot rubbish is this? There are no children in this rrroom!
Witch One It's getting stronger. Can't the rest of you smell it? Dogs' droppings.

All the Witches are sniffing now

Witches Dogs' droppings! Yes! Yes! Dogs' droppings! Dogs' droppings! Poo! Poo-oo-oo-oo-oo!

They head towards the screen

Boy is terrified

Witch One looks behind the screen

Witch One (*with a shriek*) Boy! Boy! Boy! Boy!

Pandemonium as a chase ensues. Boy runs through the Witches, desperate to escape. He runs anywhere and everywhere. The Witches chase him. He yells

Grand High Witch (*from the platform*) Grrrab it! Stop it yelling! Catch it, you idiots!

Boy is surrounded. Helpless, he submits. He is lifted up

Spying little vurm! Bring it to me.

The Witches carry him to the table and lie him or stand him on it

(*To Boy*) You stinking little carbuncle. You have observed the most
secret things. Now you must take your medicine!
Boy Help! Help! Grandmamma!
Grand High Witch Open his mouth!

*The Witches do so. Dramatically the Grand High Witch opens a formula
bottle and raises it aloft*

Five hundred doses! So strrrong vee see INSTANTANEOUS ACTION!

She pours the potion into Boy's mouth

Strange distorted alarm bells, strobing light

As the effects end, the Witches step aside, cackling manically

On the table there is no sign of Boy. Just a trembling mouse

CURTAIN

ACT II

The action is still set in the ballroom, but a giant-size section of wall, with skirting board and, perhaps, towering chair legs

As the Lights come up, a mouse scampers in and sniffs around. It is Boy — the actor dressed as a mouse. He looks about him

Boy (*calling*) Bruno! Bruno Jenkins!

No reply. Boy frisks around happily

(*To the audience*) I should be sad. I should feel desperate. I mean, I've never dreamed of being a mouse, like I've dreamed of being, say, a film star. But now that I *am* one, I'm beginning to see the advantages. I know mice sometimes get poisoned or caught in traps but boys sometimes get killed too — run over or get some awful illness. Boys have to go to school. Mice don't. Mice don't have to pass exams. When mice grow up they don't have to go out to work. Mm. It's no bad thing to be a mouse. I'm as free as William and Mary. Hope they're all right.

Bruno, dressed as a mouse, enters eating a chunk of bread

(*To Bruno*)Hallo, Bruno.

Bruno nods

What have you found?

Bruno An ancient fish paste sandwich. Pretty good. Bit pongy.

Boy Listen, Bruno. Now we're both mice, I think we ought to start thinking about the future.

Bruno stops eating

Bruno What do you mean, *we* ? The fact that you're a mouse has nothing to do with me.

Boy But you're a mouse, too, Bruno.

Bruno Don't be stupid, I'm not a mouse.

Boy I'm afraid you are, Bruno.

Bruno I most certainly am not. You're lying. I am most definitely not a mouse.

Boy Look at your paws.

Bruno You're barmy! My paws? (*He looks at them*) Aaaaah! They're all hairy. (*He feels his ears and whiskers*) Ugh! I *am* a mouse. (*He bursts into tears*)

Boy The witches did it.

Bruno I don't want to be a mouse! (*He cries more*)

Boy Don't be silly, Bruno. There are worse things than being a mouse. You can live in a hole.

Bruno I don't want to live in a hole.

Boy And you can creep into the larder at night and nibble through all the packets of biscuits and cornflakes and stuff. You can stuff yourself silly.

Bruno (*perking up*) Well, that's a thought. But how can I open the fridge door to get at the cold chicken and left overs? I do that every evening at home.

Boy Maybe your rich father will get you a special little mouse-fridge all to yourself. One you can open.

Bruno (*sudden thought*) My father. What's he going to say? And my Ma. She hates mice.

Boy I remember.

Bruno (*wailing*) What are we going to do?

Boy We'll go and see my grandmother. She'll understand. She knows all about witches.

Bruno What's all this about witches? Which witches?

Boy The witches who turned us into mice. The Grand High Witch gave you the chocolate, remember?

Bruno What, her? The miserable old bat.

Boy Yes, well. Follow me to Grandmother's room. Down the corridor,
  run like mad.
Bruno B ... b... but ...
Boy No talking. And don't let anyone see you. Don't forget that anyone
  who catches you will try to kill you!
Bruno (*terrified*) Ooooh!
Boy Come on.

*Music as they scuttle in downstage Light which holds them as the scene
changes behind them*

*They skirt imaginary walls, occasionally stopping to check the coast is
clear. They are frightened by a door slamming, echoing footsteps, and a
loud cat miaow*

Then the Lighting comes up on two giant carpeted steps

*Music continues to play as the mice arrive at the steps and consider how
to climb them*

*First Bruno helps Boy onto the first step. Then Boy tries to heave up the
unathletic Bruno. Several false starts, then Boy pulls Bruno's tail and he
finally makes it*

*As Boy contemplates the second step, Bruno notices a giant-scale sweet
wrapped in brightly coloured paper on the first step. Excited by the
thought of food he shows it to Boy. Boy mimes to him to put it down. He
does so, and helps Boy up to the second step*

*Boy now tries to hoist Bruno up. Several false starts. Boy ties their tails
together to help bring Bruno up. Eventually Bruno arrives safely*

  Boy exits as though round the corner

*Bruno goes to follow but can't resist looking down at the sweet and makes
his mind up to have it. He carefully goes back down to the first step and
grabs the sweet. But now he realizes he has to scale the second step again
—single-handed. He throws the sweet to the second step, then tries to haul
himself up. Several false starts. He even slips and hangs perilously from*

the edge. Eventually he manages to get half-way up. He then pulls his own tail to finally succeed in reaching the second step

He picks up the sweet and exits as the Lights fade

The scene changes to Grandmother's hotel bedroom. This is on a "first floor" level above the stage area. There is a bed against the wall, and a dressing table (on which the puppet mice can later act) by the door. The room opens onto a small balcony

The Lights come up on Grandmother who is sitting knitting a large sock with three needles

A female scream from outside her door makes her jump. She puts down her knitting, goes to the door and opens it

Grandmother What on earth is going on out here?
Maid (*off*) Beg your pardon, madam. I thought I saw a mouse. Aaaaah!

Her footsteps are heard as she runs away

Boy's Voice (*off*) Grandmamma! It's me, Boy! Down here.

Grandmother looks down to the floor outside the door and gasps

The witch got me.
Grandmother The witch?

Grandmother picks up the puppet Boy-Mouse and brings him into the room. She is shocked and near tears

Boy's Voice Don't cry, Grandmamma. Things could be a lot worse. I'm still alive. So's Bruno. The witch got him too. He's in the corridor.

Grandmother bends down outside the door, to pick up Bruno-Mouse. She enters the room and "puts" both mice on the dressing-table, then sits stunned

(N.B In the original production the puppet mice were "built into" the

dressing-table. Grandmother picked up another Boy-Mouse from outside the door, but, when apparently picking up Bruno-Mouse, left Boy-Mouse outside, and mimed, with her back to the audience, carrying in the two mice. Her body, in front of the dressing-table, masked the arrival of the two puppet mice, who entered from behind the dressing-table mirror)

Suddenly Bruno sees a bowl of fruit

Bruno's Voice Mm. Bananas. I like bananas. Can you peel one for me, please?

Grandmother, almost in a trance, gets up and peels one

Mm! (*He makes eating noises*)

Pause as Grandmother sits

Boy's Voice Say something, Grandmamma.
Grandmother Oh, my darling Boy, my poor sweet darling. What has she done to you?
Boy's Voice It's all right, Grandmamma, really. I'm getting used to it. It's quite fun when you get the hang of it.
Grandmother Where did it happen? Where is the witch now? Is she in the hotel?
Boy's Voice Room four-five-four. She's the Grand High Witch of all the World.
Grandmother The Grand High Witch, here?
Boy's Voice Yes. And there are masses of other witches in the hotel too.
Grandmother You don't mean they're having their Annual General Meeting here?
Boy's Voice They've had it, Grandmamma. I was there! Hiding. They call themselves the Royal Society for the Prevention of Cruelty to Children.
Grandmother Huh! Typical! And how did they catch you, my darling?
Boy's Voice They sniffed me out.
Grandmother Mm. Dogs' droppings, was it?
Boy's Voice Yes. And then the Grand High Witch demonstrated her new magic formula. It turns children into mice.
Grandmother I can see that, my darling, only too well.

Boy's Voice But Grandmamma, they plan to turn all the children of England into mice.

Grandmother The vicious creatures. That's English witches for you.

Boy's Voice We've got to stop them!

Grandmother Impossible. Witches are unstoppable. They've got you. Now they'll get the others.

Short pause

Bruno's Voice Can you peel me another banana please?

Grandmother (*peeling one*) Doesn't he ever stop eating?

Boy's Voice No. (*Suddenly*) And that's another thing Grandmamma, Bruno's parents. They don't know he's a mouse.

Grandmother I can deal with that. But stopping the witches' grand plan is another kettle of fish.

Suddenly a voice is heard from below. Grandmother and Boy react

Grand High Witch's Voice
> Down with children! Do them in!
> Boil their bones and fry their skin!

She cackles, then chants the rest, her voice getting softer. During the second half of the following chant, Boy and Grandmother continue their conversation

> Bish them, sqvish them, bash them, mash them!
> Brrreak them, shake them, slash them, smash them!

Boy's Voice It's her, Grandmamma, it's her!

Grandmother The Grand High Witch?

She goes out onto her balcony and looks down, then returns

(*Furious*) Would you believe it? The evil woman is in the room below mine!

We hear a muffled cackle from the Grand High Witch

It's a disgrace.

Boy's Voice (*after a pause*) Grandmamma. If she's down there, so is her magic formula.

Grandmother Well?

Boy's Voice (*working out his plan*) If I could only steal one tiny bottle. Five hundred doses! Works on grown-ups as well as children, she said. So who's to say it wouldn't work on *witches*. Don't you see?

Grandmother (*slowly*) I do! I do see.

Boy's Voice Witches who are meeting for dinner at eight o'clock tonight!

Grandmother Then there's no time to waste. My brilliant, darling, daring Boy.

Boy's Voice Mouse.

Grandmother Boy-Mouse, then. (*Declaiming*) For the salvation of the children of England. Action!

Exciting music as Grandmother swings into action. Meanwhile Bruno continues attacking the fruit bowl. Grandmother, having had an idea, takes her knitting and places the puppet mouse inside. She has knitted, with three needles, enough for a suitable carrier. She goes out onto the balcony and gently starts to lower the knitting by unravelling the ball of wool. Slowly 'Boy' descends until the knitting disappears from view

(*She calls*) Out you get! Hurry up!

Suddenly the sound of the room below's balcony door opening is heard

Grand High Witch's Voice Vot is this knitting-vool hanging down here?

Grandmother (*innocently*) Oh, hallo. I just dropped it over the balcony by mistake. So sorry. I've still got hold of one end, so it's all right.

She starts to pull up the wool

Grand High Witch's Voice Who vur you talking to just now? Who vur you telling to get out and hurry up?

Grandmother (*retrieving her knitting, now empty*) My little grandson. He's er ... been in the bath for ages, reading his book, the little darling. It's time he got out. Do you have any children, my dear?

Grand High Witch's Voice Certainly not!

The sound of the balcony door slamming shut

Grandmother looks concerned

Grandmother (*fervently*) Good fortune be with you, my darling Boy-Mouse.

The Lights fade

In downstage light, Boy-Mouse (the actor in mouse-costume) enters, treading gingerly

He freezes when suddenly the Grand High Witch, idly chanting, is heard, booming overhead

Grand High Witch's Voice
                    Down vith children! Do them in!
                    Boil their bones and fry their skin!
                    Bish them, sqvish them, bash them, mash them!
                    Brrreak them, shake them, slash them, smash them!

In the lull that follows, the Boy-Mouse scuttles across, but jumps as he hears a manic cackle from the Grand High Witch

He exits at speed

The Lights come up on the giant-scale underneath of the Grand High Witch's bed. This is the space between the mattress and the floor. At the back a bedspread hangs down to the floor

Boy-Mouse carefully enters under the bedspread, as though to hide. He almost backs his way in

The Grand High Witch happily hums a version of her chant. It echoes in sinister fashion. Suddenly, from behind a bedpost jumps a creature. It grabs Boy-Mouse, but not roughly. Nevertheless, Boy-Mouse jumps

Boy-Mouse Aaah!

The creature is a frog. He springs away, trembling

Hallo.

He advances. The Frog backs away

Hey, Frog, I won't hurt you.

He stretches out a paw. The Frog huddles up, enjoying the company

What are you doing here? Did the Grand High Witch magic you too?

The Frog nods

You were once a child?

The Frog nods

Have you never tried to escape?

The Frog shakes its head, fearful

You're frightened of her?

The Frog nods

So am I. Listen, Frog, do you know where she keeps her magic formula bottles?

After a thinking pause the Frog points

Boy reaches up and manages to pull down a blue bottle half his size from the bedsprings

(N.B In the original production, for practical reasons, the bottle was on the floor, in the gloom, to one side. Other bottles were painted on the flown-in flat)

Thanks, Frog.

He starts to walk and inadvertently drops the bottle

Aaah!
Grand High Witch's Voice Vot vas that? I heard a noise.

Musical sting as suddenly a corner of the bedspread lifts and the huge, upside down face of the Grand High Witch is seen peering under the bed

Boy-Mouse manages to drag the bottle into the gloom. The Frog is still visible

Vas that you, little frrroggy? Making a noise? Are you being good? Guarding my magic bottles? Are you being a good votch-frrrog? (*She cackles*) Soon I vill be giving my bottles away and you need guard them no longer.

The Frog looks chirpier

Then I vill thrrrow you out of the window and the seagulls can have you for suppertime snacks! (*She cackles*)

The Frog trembles. A knock at the bedroom door is heard

Aha. The ancient vuns come for their bottles. (*She calls*) I come.

Her face goes. The bedspread drops

Boy, with the bottle, starts to advance downstage, as though emerging from under the bed. He looks back at the trembling Frog

Come on, Frog!

To music they both escape downstage as the underbed lighting fades, walking on the spot if necessary. In the downstage area lighting covers the escape. After a circuit or two of scuttles and hops, they stop

Boy Off you go, Frog. You're free!

Boy waves farewell to Frog

They exit in different directions

The Lights fade. Into a pool of light steps the Head Waiter, banging a gong

Head Waiter Ladies and gentlemen. Dinner is served.

Music as the Lights come up on the hotel restaurant where a large table (for the Witches) is set upstage centre. We imagine the kitchen is situated off to one side. On the other side is Grandmother's table. Other tables are visible, but do not obscure the witches' table

Head Waiter enters the scene

A Waiter and a Waitress hover. Head Waiter checks all is ready

He then exits to deposit his dinner gong offstage

A group of Diners enter

(N.B In the original production, because not all the Witches could be accommodated at the large table, three of them doubled as ordinary diners)

The Waiter approaches and leads them to a table. The Waitress begins to take their orders

Grandmother enters

She holds, carefully, her large handbag in which are supposedly the two mice. She waits until the Waiter approaches

Waiter Good-evening, madam.
Grandmother Good-evening.
Waiter Your table is this way.
Grandmother Thank you.

He leads her to her table, set with two chairs. She sits on one and carefully places her handbag on the other

The Waiter departs to lay plates on the Witches' table

The Head Waiter enters and approaches Grandmother with his notepad and pencil

Head Waiter Good-evening, madam.
Grandmother Good-evening.
Head Waiter Where is the young gentleman tonight?
Grandmother He's not feeling quite himself. He's staying in his room.
Head Waiter I'm sorry to hear that. Now, this evening, to start with there is green pea soup, and for the main course you have a choice of either grilled fillet of sole or roast lamb.
Grandmother Pea soup and lamb for me, please.
Head Waiter Thank you, madam.
Grandmother Thank you!

The Head Waiter leaves, heading for the kitchen

Grandmother surreptitiously speaks into her handbag

Grandmother Ready, my darling? Have you got the bottle?
Boy's Voice Yes. Grandmamma, what's the time?
Grandmother (*checking her watch*) It's five minutes to eight. We're just in time.

She carefully lowers the handbag to the floor, behind the table

Grandmother Out you get. Stand by. Good luck!

She brings the handbag up to the table

Bruno's Voice (*in the handbag*) I'm starving!
Grandmother Quiet, Bruno. Have a bread roll.

She takes a roll from a side-plate and pops it in the handbag

Bruno's Voice It's got no butter!
Grandmother (*loudly*) Shut up!

*The Waitress nearby hears and looks round, startled, at Grandmother,
who smiles sweetly*

The Waitress starts to exit

Grandmother checks the coast is clear, then looks down

Go!

The Waitress freezes as the Lights change

*A puppet Boy-Mouse with a formula bottle scuttles all the way across
the stage and exits*

The Lights change back. The Waitress continues her exit

The Head Waiter enters with a bowl. He goes to Grandmother

Head Waiter Your green pea soup, madam.
Grandmother Thank you. It smells most appetising.

Eight o'clock chimes, followed by music

*The Witches enter, led by the Grand High Witch wearing her face mask.
They behave very obsequiously*

Head Waiter Good-evening, ladies.
Grand High Witch Good-evening.
Head Waiter Your table is this way.

*The Head Waiter and the Waiter help them into their chairs. Grandmother
watches. When all are settled the Head Waiter speaks*

Tonight, ladies, there is green pea soup to start with, and for the main
course you have a choice of either grilled fillet of sole or roast lamb.

*His words are almost drowned by the rising music. The Lights snap down.
Loud kitchen noises as, on the side of the stage opposite Grandmother's*

table, a small kitchen set appears. It is pushed on by the Head Chef and the Second Chef. It consists of a dresser with a work-top, pans and kitchen utensils and a counter with an electric hob and saucepans

The Lights snap up as the two Chefs burst into activity. The Head Chef stirs the soup and the Second Chef bangs a slice of meat with a rolling pin. Suddenly they freeze, as the focus changes to the top of the dresser

Music as a puppet Boy-Mouse appears holding the formula bottle. He negotiates a pot or two. Hiding behind a pot, he peeps round and backs away again

The Lights come back on the Chefs. They unfreeze and start stirring and banging again

The Waiter hurries in

Waiter (*shouting*) Two lamb for table four!
Head Chef Two lamb for table four!
Second Chef Two lamb for table four!

Working as a double act, they slap two plates on the counter

Head Chef }
Second Chef } (*together*)   Meat!

They slap a slice on each plate

Second Chef } (*together, proudly*)   Meat!
Head Chef }
Second Chef Peas!
Head Chef Peas!

They plop a handful of peas on each plate

Second Chef } (*together, proudly*)   Peas!
Head Chef }
Head Chef Carrots!
Second Chef Carrots!

They chuck a handful of carrots on each plate

Second Chef ⎱
Head Chef   ⎰ *(together, proudly)*   Carrots!
Second Chef Gravy!
Head Chef Gravy!

He tips a gravy boat. It is empty

  No gravy!
Second Chef No gravy!
Head Chef *(idea)* Do-it-yourself gravy!
Second Chef Do-it-yourself gravy!

*Each takes a plate and spits on it. Then they plump up the food with their
fingers*

Second Chef ⎱
Head Chef   ⎰ *(together, proudly)*   Two lamb for table four!
Second Chef ⎱ *(together to the waiter, shouting)* Two lamb for table
Head Chef   ⎰ four!!
Waiter *(taking the plates)* Two lamb for table four!

  He exits, nearly bumping into the Head Waiter as he enters

Head Waiter *(shouting)* Everyone in the big RSPCC party wants the
soup!

  He exits

Head Chef Soup for the big party!
Second Chef Soup for the big party!
Head Chef In the silver soup-tureen!
Second Chef In the silver soup-tureen!

*They find it under the counter and place it on the work-top right under
where the Boy-Mouse is hiding*

As they return to their counter, suddenly the action freezes. The Lights focus on the puppet Boy-Mouse. Music as he pushes through the pans on a shelf and pours green liquid from the bottle down into the soup-tureen. The puppet Boy-Mouse retreats

The action unfreezes

Head Chef Pour in the soup!
Second Chef Pour in the soup!

They take the saucepan and pour soup into the tureen. The soup can be imaginary if the pouring is masked by the saucepan

Head Chef } *(together)* } Soup for the big party! *(They shout)*
Second Chef } Soup for the big party!

The Head Waiter enters with a trolley

The Head Chef and the Second Chef place the soup-tureen on the trolley

Head Waiter *(as he goes)* Soup for the big party!

Head Waiter exits pushing the trolley

Suddenly an enamel plate or somesuch falls off the top of the dresser, hitting the Second Chef and revealing the Boy-Mouse, who has inadvertently dislodged it

Second Chef What was that?

He looks round and up

Hey, look! A mouse! A mouse!
Head Chef Where, where?
Second Chef There, there!

Exciting chase music as the Chefs grab a rolling pin and ladle and try to wallop the Boy-Mouse, who quickly hides behind the pot

He's hiding! He's hiding!
Head Chef There he goes!

They follow the imaginary progress of the mouse down the side of the dresser, across to behind the counter. Slapstick fun as the Chefs try to whack the mouse but only succeed in whacking each other and bumping into each other

Take that!
Second Chef Ow! Take that!
Head Chef Ow!

Suddenly the Second Chef freezes in horror

Second Chef Eeeeee!
Head Chef What is it?
Second Chef Jeepers creepers! It's gone up my trouser leg! Ah! Ah! Oo! Oo!

He comes out from behind the counter, jumping up and down, slapping his trouser leg

Holy smoke! It's going all the way up! Ah! Oo! Help!

Now he is jumping up and down as though he is standing on hot bricks

Help! Help!

He stops suddenly

It's in my knickers! There's a mouse running around in my flaming knickers! Aaaaah!
Head Chef Quick! Get 'em off!

He attacks the Second Chef, trying to get his trousers off. The Second Chef resists

Second Chef Stop it! Stop it! You're tickling!

He giggles hysterically

Head Chef Off! Off!

Suddenly the Second Chef's trousers drop revealing funny underwear

Black-out

Music as the scene clears. The Lights come up on the restaurant as we left it with Grandmother at her table and the Witches awaiting their soup

   The Waitress enters with rolls for the other diners

Bruno's Voice Can I have another roll please?
Grandmother (*loudly*) Quiet, Bruno!

The Waitress hears and looks, startled, at Grandmother who smiles sweetly

   The Waitress exits

Grandmother puts another roll in her handbag

The Head Waiter approaches Grandmother, sees her apparently taking the roll, but discreetly ignores it

Head Waiter Have you finished your green pea soup, madam?
Grandmother Thank you, it was delicious.
Head Waiter Thank *you*, madam. I'm glad you enjoyed it.

   He starts to exit towards the kitchen, then freezes as the Lights change

Suddenly the puppet Boy-Mouse, without the formula bottle, scuttles from the kitchen side across the stage towards Grandmother's table, apparently arriving behind it

   The Lights change back. The Head Waiter unfreezes and exits

Boy's Voice Grandmamma, I'm back! Mission accomplished!

Grandmother (*'picking him up' and hiding him behind a menu, then revealing him to the audience*) Well *done*, my darling. Well done, you.
Boy's Voice Have the witches arrived, Grandmamma?
Grandmother They're over there, my darling. Look!

She positions the menu to give Boy-Mouse a view

Music as the Head Waiter, Waiter and Waitress enter pushing the soup-tureen on its trolley

Head Waiter Ladies, your green pea soup.

They arrive at the Witches' table and start to serve it as the focus returns to Grandmother's table

Boy's Voice They're going to drink it, Grandmamma, they're going to drink it!

The Boy-Mouse bobs up and down

Grandmother Shhh! Keep still. And cross your fingers.
Boy's Voice I haven't got any fingers to cross.
Grandmother Sorry. (*She smiles*)

Mr and Mrs Jenkins enter, scanning the restaurant. They see Grandmother and head towards her

Boy's Voice Look out, Grandmamma. It's Bruno's parents.

Grandmother rearranges the menu to hide the puppet Boy-Mouse. Meanwhile the Witches start drinking their soup. The Head Waiter, Waiter and Waitress hover

Mr Jenkins Where's that grandson of yours?
Mrs Jenkins We reckon he's up to something with our …
Mr Jenkins
Mrs Jenkins } (*together*) { Bruno.
Mrs Jenkins Some devilment.

Mr Jenkins The little beggar's not turned up for his supper. Most unlike him.

Mrs Jenkins Most unlike him.

Grandmother I agree. He has a very healthy appetite.

Mrs Jenkins How do you know? Have you seen him? Where is he?

Grandmother I'm afraid I have some rather alarming news for you. He's in my handbag.

She takes hold of it. Mr and Mrs Jenkins can't believe their ears

Mr Jenkins What the heck d'you mean he's in your handbag?

Mrs Jenkins Are you trying to be funny?

Grandmother There's nothing funny about it. Your son has been rather drastically altered.

Mr Jenkins ⎰ (*together*) ⎱ Altered?
Mrs Jenkins ⎱   ⎰

Mr Jenkins What the devil do you mean?

Grandmother My own grandson actually saw them doing it to him.

Mr Jenkins Saw *who* doing *what* to him, for heaven's sake?

Grandmother Saw the witches turning him into a mouse.

The Jenkins' mouths gape

Mrs Jenkins Call the manager, dear. Have this mad woman thrown out of the hotel.

Grandmother (*calmly*) Bruno is a mouse.

Mr Jenkins He most certainly is not a mouse!

Suddenly Bruno-Mouse pops his head out of the handbag

Bruno's Voice Oh yes I am! Hallo Pa, hallo Ma!

Mrs Jenkins nearly screams. She and Mr Jenkins back off nervously, horrified

Mr Jenkins B-b-b-b...

Bruno's Voice Don't worry, Pa. It's not as bad as all that. Just so long as the cat doesn't get me.

Mr Jenkins But I can't have a mouse for a son!

Grandmother You've got one. Be nice to him.
Mrs Jenkins (*approaching with difficulty*) My poor baby! Who did this?

Mrs Jenkins picks up Bruno in the handbag, trying to hide her distaste

Grandmother That woman over there.

She points to the Grand High Witch

Black dress. Finishing her soup.
Mr Jenkins She's RSPCC. The chairwoman.
Grandmother No. She's the Grand High Witch of all the World.
Mrs Jenkins You mean *she* did it? That skinny woman over there?
Mr Jenkins What a nerve. I'll make her pay through the nose. I'll have
my lawyers on to her for this.

He turns towards the Grand High Witch

Grandmother I wouldn't do anything rash. That woman has magic
powers. She might turn *you* into something. A cockroach, perhaps.
Mr Jenkins Turn *me* into a cockroach? I'd like to see her try!

*He sets off again. But he is stopped in his tracks by a very loud alarm bell.
The lighting focuses on the Witches' table. It should create an eerie
atmosphere. It is suggested that all the following action is performed in
slow motion against a background of distorted clock and bell sounds*

*The Grand High Witch leaps in the air, onto her chair, then onto the table.
She clutches her throat, aware that she has been poisoned. Smoke begins
to swirl around the Witches' table.Witch One and other Witches start to
leap up on the table too, others simply stand. All writhe about waving their
arms. The other Diners, the Head Waiter, Waitress and Waiter, as well as
Grandmother and Mr and Mrs Jenkins watch the Witches' behaviour in
awed amazement. The Grand High Witch climbs down from the table. She
realizes the soup is responsible for her behaviour and approaches the
tureen in fury. The Head Waiter, terrified, pushes the tureen trolley
towards her in self-defence. The Grand High Witch avoids the trolley,
which collides into Mr Jenkins. As the other Witches start to 'shrink', still
writhing helplessly, the Grand High Witch advances downstage. She*

removes her wig and face mask, revealing her horrid face to the audience, then turns upstage. The other Diners, the Head Waiter, Waitress, Waiter, Grandmother, Mr and Mrs Jenkins react in horror. The Head Waiter and Mr Jenkins advance towards the Grand High Witch, who evades them, but finds her only escape route is over the trolley. She climbs up on it. The Head Waiter and Mr Jenkins try to reach her, forcing her to step into the tureen

Everyone watches as, screaming in a nightmarish echo, the Grand High Witch descends into the tureen and disappears, a desperate hand being the last part of her to go. If a tureen trolley is not possible, the Grand High Witch could disappear with the other Witches, but to give her a more horrible end than the others is satisfying to the audience

Amazed, the others look on as the Head Waiter picks up the wig and face mask that the Grand High Witch has dropped, and shows them around. Mr Jenkins looks into the tureen and a mouse, covered in green pea soup, slowly appears from the tureen, looking at him and quivering with rage

As Mr Jenkins and the Head Waiter clear the trolley away, we become aware that all the other Witches have vanished

Then puppet mice appear from behind the table and, if possible, in other places. The Witches have all been turned to mice. As the music rises and the Lights fade, Grandmother holds up the Boy-Mouse puppet in triumph and Mrs Jenkins shows Bruno-Mouse the successful conclusion of the Boy-Mouse's plan

After a fade to Black-out, a pool of light reveals Grandmother holding the puppet Boy-Mouse

Grandmother The Boy-Mouse had saved the children of England. I took him home to Norway where I could best take care of him.

The Lights come up on Grandmother's parlour in Norway. There is now a small ladder stretching from the floor to the tabletop

Grandmother crosses to her parlour and places the puppet Boy-Mouse on the table, while picking up her embroidery. She sits in her chair

*If the puppet cannot be operated from under the table, Grandmother could
simply sit with the puppet Boy-Mouse in her arms*

The clocks ticks

Boy's Voice Grandmamma, has the Grand High Witch really gone
forever?
Grandmother Yes, my darling. But Grand High Witches are like queen
bees. There's always another one to take over. Let's hope there are
always people like you brave enough to foil their wicked plans.
Boy's Voice Even if they end up as mice?
Grandmother Even if they end up as mice.

Pause

Boy's Voice Can I ask you something, Grandmamma?
Grandmother Anything.
Boy's Voice How long does a mouse live?
Grandmother Not very long, I'm afraid. Just a few years.

Pause

Boy's Voice And how much longer will you live, Grandmamma?
Grandmother Just a few years.
Boy's Voice Good. I'll be a very old mouse and you'll be a very old
grandmother and we'll both die together.
Grandmother That would be perfect.

Pause

My darling, are you sure you don't mind being a mouse for the rest of
your life?
Boy's Voice I don't mind at all. It doesn't matter who you are or what you
look like so long as somebody loves you.

*Grandmother's hand and the puppet Boy-Mouse's paw meet. They remain
silent and happy together as the music rises and the Lights fade*

CURTAIN

FURNITURE AND PROPERTY LIST

ACT I

On stage: Easy chair
Small table with a lamp. *On it*: large tome

Personal   **Grandmother**: thin black cigar, box of matches, watch
(worn throughout)
Lawyer: briefcase, document

During Black-out on page 5

Strike: Easy chair
Small table

As Grandmother exits on page 6

On stage: Hammer
Nails
Plank

Off stage: Torch: **Grandmother**

Personal: **Display Witch**: handbag. *In it*: thin green snake

During Black-out page 8

Strike: Hammer
Nails
Plank

Set: Armchair

As music plays on page 9

Strike: Armchair

Off stage   Paper bag containing a jam doughnut (**Mrs Jenkins**)

Personal: **Bruno**: magnifying glass, cream bun
                     Grand High Witch: Bar of chocolate

During Black-out on page 14

Set: Mirrors
                     Chandelier
                     Raised platform
                     Folding screen
                     Door with key
                     Small table
                     Board or scroll with *"Formula Eighty-Six Delayed-Action
                         Mouse-Maker"* written on followed by the recipe
                     Gong

Off stage: Piece of cake (**Boy**)

Personal: **Witches**: handbags containing pads and pencils
                     Grand High Witch: potion bottle, tiny bottle

ACT II

On stage: Nil

Off stage: Chunk of bread (**Bruno**)

During Lighting change on page 28

Set: Two giant carpeted steps. *On the first step*: giant scale sweet
                         wrapped in coloured paper

During Black-out on page 29

On stage: Bed
                     Dressing-table
                     Piece of knitting with three needles
                     Bowl of fruit including bananas

During Lighting change on page 33

Set: Small blue bottle

During Black-out on page 36

On stage: Large table UC
                Smaller tables positioned so as not to obscure witches table.
                On each table: bread rolls on side-plates, menus

Off stage: Notepad and pencil (**Head Waiter**)
                Gong (**Head Waiter**)
                Plates (**Waiter**)
                Bowl (**Head Waiter**)

Personal: **Grandmother**: large handbag

During Black-out on page 38

Set: Kitchen dresser with a work-top.*On it*: pots and pans,
                rolling pin, ladle *etc*. *In it*: silver soup tureen
                Counter with electric hob. *On it*: saucepans containing
                carrots, peas, slices of meat, gravy boat

Off stage: Trolley (**Head Waiter**)
                Basket of bread rolls (**Waitress**)

During Black-out on page 43

Strike: Kitchen dresser and counter

During Black-out page 47

On stage: Grandmother's parlour in Norway as Act I
                Small table. *On it*: piece of embroidery
                Small ladder stretching from the floor to the table top

LIGHTING PLOT

Property fittings required: chandelier (optional)
Various interior and exterior settings

To open: Curtain rises on a darkened stage

Cue 1	Sudden screech of brakes. Crash.	(Page 1)
	Snap on spot on Boy. Bring up Lights on Grandmother's parlour	
Cue 2	**Grandmother** opens a large tome. Music plays	(Page 3)
	Snap on spot on Display Witch	
Cue 3	**Display Witch** cackles menacingly and disappears	(Page 4)
	Fade on Display Witch	
Cue 4	**Grandmother**: "No time to waste."	(Page 5)
	Fade to black-out	
Cue 5	Seagulls' cries and sound of sea	(Page 5)
	Bring up lights on ship's rail	
Cue 6	**Boy**: " ... building at the bottom of the garden ..."	(Page 6)
	Lights come up on the tree-house	
Cue 7	**Tree-House Witch** leaves, cackling horribly	(Page 7)
	Fade to night-time effect	
Cue 8	**Boy**: "I've seen a witch." A cackle echoes	(Page 8)
	Fade lights to black-out	
Cue 9	When ready	(Page 8)
	Bring up lights on a small area downstage	
Cue 10	**Boy**: "...Norway for the holidays, she fell ill, very ill."	(Page 8)
	Bring up lights on another downstage area	
Cue 11	Scene changes to the imposing front door of the hotel	(Page 9)
	Bring up lights on hotel	
Cue 12	**Bruno**:"You bet I'll be there!"	(Page 14)
	Fade lights on Bruno	

Cue 13 | When ready | (Page 14)
Bring up lights on Ballroom

Cue 14 | **Boy:** "One, two, three, hup! Bravo!! " | (Page 15)
Ballroom is flooded with light from chandelier

Cue 15 | **Grand High Witch:** "Vee have ignition." An alarm rings (Page 22)
Strange lighting effects

Cue 16 | **Grand High Witch** pours the potion into **Boy**'s mouth | (Page 24)
Strobing light

ACT II

To open: Bring up lights on Ballroom (Giant Skirting Board)

Cue 17 | **Boy:** "Come on." | (Page 28)
Bring up lights on downstage; fade lights upstage

Cue 18 | Door slams, footsteps echo and a loud cat miaow | (Page 28)
Bring up lights on two giant carpeted steps

Cue 19 | **Bruno** picks up the sweet and exits | (Page 29)
Fade to black-out

Cue 20 | When ready | (Page 29)
Bring up lights on Grandmother's hotel bedroom

Cue 21 | **Grandmother:** "...my darling Boy-Mouse." | (Page 33)
Fade to black-out

Cue 22 | When ready | (Page 33)
Bring up lights downstage

Cue 23 | **Boy** exits at speed | (Page 33)
Bring up lights on giant-scale underneath of Grand High Witch's bed

Cue 24 | **Boy** and **Frog** escape downstage. Music plays | (Page 35)
Fade underbed lighting to black-out

Cue 25 | **Boy** and **Frog** exit in different directions | (Page 35)
Fade to black-out

Cue 26   When ready   (Page 36)
           Snap on spot on Head Waiter

Cue 27   **Head Waiter:** "Ladies and gentlemen. Dinner is served." (Page 36)
           Bring up lights on hotel restaurant

Cue 28   **Grandmother:**"Go!"   (Page 38)
           Lights change for Puppet Boy-Mouse cross-over

Cue 29   Puppet Boy-Mouse exits   (Page 38)
           Revert to previous lighting

Cue 30   **Head Waiter:** "... or sole or roast lamb."   (Page 38)
           Snap off lights

Cue 31   Two Chefs burst into activity   (Page 39)
           Snap on lights on Chefs

Cue 32   **Second Chef** and **Head Chef** freeze   (Page 39)
           Focus lights on top of dresser

Cue 33   **Boy-Mouse** peeps around and backs away again   (Page 39)
           Focus lights on Chefs

Cue 34   **Head Chef** and **Second Chef** freeze   (Page 40)
           Focus lights on puppet Boy-Mouse

Cue 35   Puppet Boy-Mouse peeps round the pot and backs away (Page 39)
           Bring up lights on the Chefs

Cue 36   Suddenly **Second Chef's** trousers drop   (Page 43)
           Black-out

Cue 37   Scene clears. Music plays   (Page 43)
           Bring up lights on restaurant

Cue 38   **Head Waiter** starts to exit into the kitchen. He freezes   (Page 43)
           Lights change for puppet Boy-Mouse cross-over

Cue39   Puppet Boy-Mouse arrives behind Grandmother's table (Page 43)
           Revert to previous lighting

Cue 40   **Mr Jenkins** sets off again. Very loud alarm bell   (Page 46)
           Focus lights on Witches' table creating an eerie atmosphere

Cue 41   Puppet mice appear from behind the table. Music rises   (Page 47)
            Fade lights

Cue 42   **Mrs Jenkins** shows Bruno-Mouse the conclusion   (Page 47)
            Fade to black-out. Bring up spot on Grandmother

Cue 43   **Grandmother**: " ...where I could best take care of him." (Page 47)
            Bring up lights on Grandmother's parlour in Norway

Cue 44   **Grandmother's** hand and the **Boy-Mouse's** paw meet   (Page 48)
            Fade lights

EFFECTS PLOT

ACT I

Cue 1　As House Lights go down　　　　　　　　　　(Page 1)
Gentle purr of a car engine. Volume increases to an engine roar

Cue 2　Curtain rises　　　　　　　　　　　　　(Page 1)
Sudden screech of brakes. A crash

Cue 3　**Grandmother** leads **Boy** to her chair　　　(Page 2)
A clock ticks

Cue 4　**Grandmother**: "No time to waste." Lights fade　(Page 5)
Ship's hooter fills the air. Seagulls' cries. Sound of sea

Cue 5　Lights come up on the tree-house　　　　　(Page 6)
Birdsong

Cue 6　**Tree-House Witch** traces the scent　　　　(Page 6)
Birdsong stops

Cue 7　**Tree-House Witch** leaves cackling. Lights fade　(Page 5)
An owl hoots

Cue 8　Scene changes to front door of the hotel　　(Page 9)
Traffic noises

Cue 9　Staring at **Witch Two**, **Grand High Witch** gestures　(Page 17)
Sparks fly. Smoke rises

Cue 10　**Grand High Witch**: "Vee have ignition."　　(Page 22)
Alarm rings

Cue 11　**Grand High Witch**: "A lovely little MOUSE!"　(Page 22)
Flash. Smoke

Cue 12　**Grand High Witch** pours the potion into **Boy's** mouth
Strange distorted alarm bells　　　　　　　(Page 23)

Cue 13　When ready　　　　　　　　　　　　(Page 25)
End effects

ACT II

MADE AND PRINTED IN GREAT BRITAIN BY
LATIMER TREND & COMPANY LTD PLYMOUTH

MADE IN ENGLAND